Indian Myths

For Max Thomas Shackle - S.H

Published by Evans Brothers Limited
2A Portman Mansions
Chiltern Street
London W1U 6NR

© Evans Brothers Limited 2005
First published 2005
Printed in China

British Library Cataloguing in Publication Data

Husain, Shahrukh
  Indian Myths (Stories from ancient civilisations)
  1. Legends - India - Juvenile literature
  2. Mythology, Indic - Juvenile literature
  I. Title
  398. 2'0954

  ISBN 0 237 52448 1
   13-digit ISBN (from 1 Jan 2007) 978 0 237 52448 7

CREDITS
Editor: Julia Bird
Design: Robert Walster
Artworks: Bee Willey
Production: Jenny Mulvanny

STORIES FROM ANCIENT CIVILISATIONS

Indian Myths

Shahrukh Husain
and Bee Willey

Evans

Introduction

Myths are probably the earliest stories ever told. People in ancient times used them to explain all that was important in life – how the universe was created, how the stars, sun, moon and planets appeared in the sky. To them, these elements were gods whom they worshipped and whom they believed controlled their lives. They wanted to keep the gods happy to gain their blessings.

Myths are usually about important matters like birth, death and the afterlife, and tend to have a moral. In the story of Shantanu (see pages 20-22), the Indian goddess Ganga explains the belief that souls who have sinned are reborn until they live a sin-free life. After that their spirit is set free, never again to be burdened with a body which feels pain. The god Vishnu was reborn ten times to complete his work in the human world. This continuous cycle of life is also true of the Indian cosmos, which is constantly destroyed and recreated. The supreme Hindu gods, old and new, consisted of two main triads, or threesomes, reflecting the three vital aspects of the universe – creation, survival and rebirth.

The early Indian gods were nature gods. The ancient Indians made offerings to please them so that they would be rewarded with plenty of water and sun to bring good harvests. These people often travelled huge distances, looking for new lands to settle. They took their own gods and myths with them on their journeys. When they settled somewhere new, an exchange took place. They introduced their gods to the local people and, in turn, began to worship some of theirs. So over time more myths were added to each story-telling tradition, and sometimes the same gods were called different names as old stories blended with new ones. In India, Indra, the supreme god of the prehistoric Indians, lost much of his importance over time. He was replaced by the new god of the fields and hillsides, Krishna. Their rivalry in myths such as the lifting of Govardhan (see page 15) shows how the worshippers of the new gods believed their own gods to be superior. On the other hand, another prehistoric god, Brahma, was easily absorbed into the new family of Indian gods where he worked alongside Vishnu, as we see in the myth of the recreation of the world. Over the centuries, the new gods gained prominence and the female divine, Shakti, became more widely worshipped, particularly in the warlike form of Kali.

Indian myths are mostly about the constant war between good and evil. They also teach that it is important to worship the gods and that everything in nature is cyclical. In its early history, India was often invaded and this is reflected in the two great epics, the Ramayana and the Mahabharata. The sources of Indian stories are many, but they are hard to date. The Rigveda, which tells us about the early nature gods, Indra and his family, was compiled between 1500 and 900 BCE. The Ramayana is thought to have been composed around 1000 BCE, and the Mahabharata a hundred years later in 900 BCE. The myths exist in many different Indian languages and leave a vivid account of the way of life in India across a long time-span. The religious beliefs set out in the books are still practised today.

Contents

The Cosmic Ocean

This story describes how two of the best-known Indian gods, Brahma and Vishnu, remake the cosmos again and again. Hindus believe people are continually reborn in other forms, so death is a stage of life, not the end. The world is also continually recreated in the same way.

Vasuki was the king of the serpents, who were demi-gods and lived in the dark underworld, known as Patal. Cobras are still respected all over India and on one day of the year, Nag Panchami, saucers of milk are left out to feed them. Vasuki is also known as Shesh Nag.

THE GREAT GOD VISHNU, PRESERVER OF THE UNIVERSE, SURVEYED THE WORLD. All seemed peaceful.

'It is time to rest,' Vishnu decided, raising his hand to summon Vasuki, chief of the serpents. Vasuki arrived, dressed in magnificent robes of purple, wearing rows of glimmering white pearls, and offered his wide back as a bed to the god. Vishnu lay down on Vasuki's back and the great cobra spread his thousand hoods to shade the god as he prepared to float on the Cosmic Ocean.

Vishnu sank into a deep sleep that would last the whole night. But one night of the gods is many millennia for humans. And while Vishnu slept, the whole universe was destroyed and recreated. It began as Vasuki spat out a special poison which turned into a fire, which made the universe slowly burn and sink into the Cosmic Ocean.

But Brahma, the god of creation, was ready. He placed a golden seed in the swirling waters of the Ocean and waited for it to grow into an egg. When the egg hatched, Brahma himself emerged from it and sat on a lotus flower in the centre to create the new cosmos. He raised one half of the egg and made it the sky. The second half, he placed beneath him, creating the Earth. The golden yolk in the centre became the radiant sun, Surya.

When Vishnu finally stirred and awoke, he would discover a whole new cosmos and his work for the day would begin again.

The Birth of Indra

Ancient Indians claimed they did not know how the world began, only that Dyaus-Pitar (Sky), and his wife Prithvi (Earth), created the nature gods. These included Ushas (dawn) and Vayu (wind), but also Vritra, the serpent of drought and famine. The fight between Vritra and Indra in this myth represents the eternal struggle of farming communities against the harsh forces of nature.

THE PLANTS AND FIELDS HAD WITHERED AWAY. It made Prithvi, the Earth, sad and angry.

'Vritra is taking away the water from the world,' she told Dyaus-Pitar, the Sky. 'We must stop him.'

She blinked and suddenly, two young men lay sleeping before her. One sat up. He had four arms. One arm held a sword, a second wielded Vajra, his thunderbolt-spear, and the third, a rainbow with which to shoot arrows. His fourth arm was free to be used when he faced Vritra, the serpent of drought and famine.

'This is our son Indra,' Prithvi smiled at Dyaus-Pitar. 'He is master of the atmosphere and protector of harvests. His sleeping brother is Agni, god of fire.'

Before confronting Vritra, Indra went first to the nature spirits, known as the Gandharvas, who made him soma – a magical juice which gave its drinkers enormous strength.

Indra drank the juice until he felt power course through his body. Then he leapt on his chariot and soared through the skies on his mission. Vritra had hidden himself in distant fortresses made of clouds and mist, but Indra was not put off. He destroyed one fortress after another until, at last, he cornered Vritra.

The fearsome serpent snarled and lunged at him. But Indra was ready. He crouched until Vritra was close, then flung Vajra vigorously. Vritra gave a great roar. His belly split, releasing the waters of Earth, which flooded out into the clouds and cascaded down to Earth. At last, years of drought and famine came to an end. The land grew lush, crops flourished and people could eat again. Vritra lived on in the skies, threatening to bring drought another day. But Indra would always be ready for him.

This story is from the Rigveda, a book of hymns compiled between 1500-900 BCE. Its gods symbolise nature and are called the Vedic gods. The three most important were Indra, god of fertility and rain, Surya, the Sun, and Indra's twin, Agni, who was fire. All three were worshipped by ancient Indians who lived off the land.

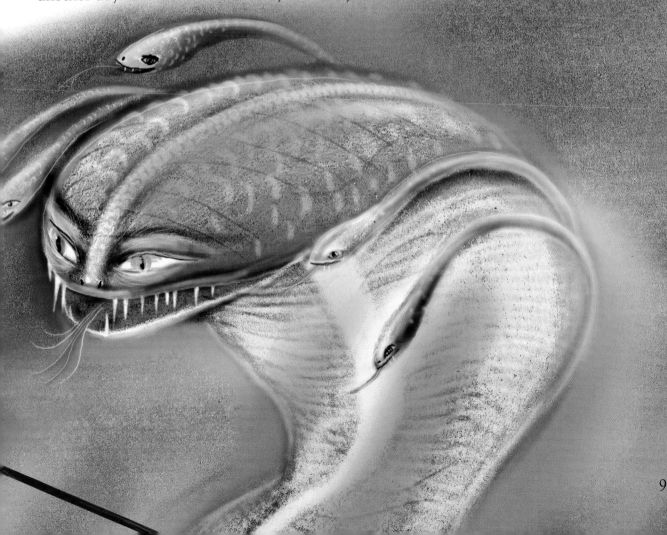

The Churning
of the Ocean of Milk

The Indian gods fought a constant battle with the demons. The demons devoted years of prayer to gain powers to use against the gods. The god Shiva insisted the prayers of worshippers, even evil ones, had to be rewarded. So the world was always in danger from these evil creatures.

INDRA, KING OF THE GODS, WAS GROWING WEAK. 'We need Vishnu's help to make him stronger,' the anxious gods decided. 'If we fail, the demons will triumph and make the world an evil place.'

The gods set off for Vaikuntha, Vishnu's heaven.

'The Elixir of Life will increase your strength fourfold,' Vishnu told Indra. 'To get it, you must churn the Ocean of Milk. Use Vasuki, king of the serpents, as a rope. Mount Mandan will be your churning stick. You will pull from one side and the demons from the other.'

'The demons?' Indra gasped. 'But we can't let them have the elixir. They'll become even stronger!'

Vishnu chuckled. 'You need their strength. I will make sure they don't drink the elixir.'

The gods and the demons gathered around the Ocean of Milk. Each side held firmly onto Vasuki and pulled. The mountain swivelled from side to side. The ocean waves rose, making the milky water froth and foam. Faster and faster they pulled, as if in a tug of war. The mountain spun so furiously, it bored deep into the ground. Vishnu turned a part of himself into a large tortoise and stood beneath the mountain to hold up the world. As the churning continued, a cow appeared from the foaming surface of the ocean.

'This is Surabhi, the cow of plenty,' Vishnu said. 'She can grant all wishes.' As the gods helped Surabhi out, the ocean turned into a frothing whirlpool.

There were many demon races - Asuras, Daityas and Danavas. They included giants and ogres, as well as goblins, vampires and ghosts, and their aim was to take over the world and destroy all the good in it. They worshipped Shiva, god of destruction, the third god of the triad of Brahma, Vishnu and Shiva.

One by one, miraculous creatures and objects emerged from the frothy water. First came the Apsaras, heavenly dancing maidens. The goddess of good fortune, Lakshmi, appeared and Vishnu decided to take her as a wife. The crescent moon flew out and attached itself to Shiva's hair. Then came poison, which Shiva swallowed before the demons could reach it. It stained his throat deep blue.

At last, an old physician rose to the surface. He was holding up a chalice which contained the Elixir of Life! The demons and the gods rushed to get to it first. But the demons were stronger and surged together towards the physician. Suddenly, they heard exquisite music. The Apsaras were dancing. The demons were enchanted.

The next moment, the gods had taken possession of the chalice. Vishnu had kept his promise to take care of the demons and Indra's strength was restored.

Vedic and Hindu Gods

The gods of Indian myths can be divided into the old gods who come from the Vedas, and the new Hindu gods who rose to popularity later and remain dominant to this day.

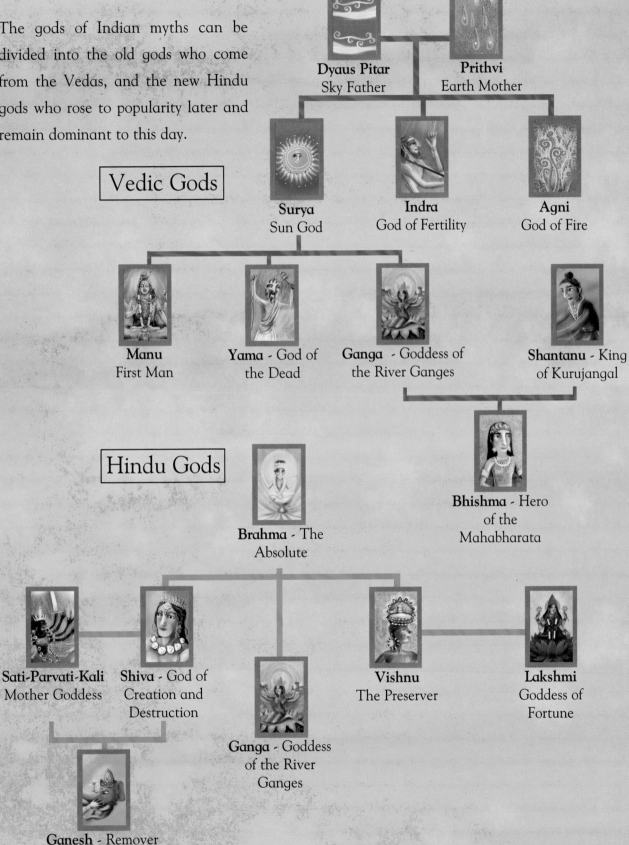

Vedic Gods

Dyaus Pitar
Sky Father

Prithvi
Earth Mother

Surya
Sun God

Indra
God of Fertility

Agni
God of Fire

Manu
First Man

Yama - God of
the Dead

Ganga - Goddess of
the River Ganges

Shantanu - King
of Kurujangal

Bhishma - Hero
of the
Mahabharata

Hindu Gods

Brahma - The
Absolute

Sati-Parvati-Kali
Mother Goddess

Shiva - God of
Creation and
Destruction

Ganga - Goddess
of the River
Ganges

Vishnu
The Preserver

Lakshmi
Goddess of
Fortune

Ganesh - Remover
of Obstacles

Krishna, God of the Fields

This story of the birth of Krishna comes from a book called the Bhagavada Purana, which is believed to have been written around 1000 CE. Krishna, the flute-player, is one of the most popular Hindu gods. Songs are still sung all over India about his antics as a naughty child, getting milkmaids into trouble by drinking their milk and eating up their freshly churned butter.

Krishna was the blue-grey of a rain cloud. This was probably because he took over the role of bringing rain and keeping the fields fertile from Indra. As a god, he wore a gold necklace and a crown decorated with a peacock feather.

KING KANS OF MATHURA WAS AN EVIL SORCERER AND A CRUEL KING.

One day, he summoned his guards to him.

'Imprison my sister Devaki and her husband Vasudev,' he ordered. 'My magic tells me that their eighth son will kill me and take away my kingdom.'

Devaki and Vasudev were locked into their home and, one by one, Devaki's sons were killed at birth. Only the seventh, Balrama, was saved because Vasudev managed to spirit him away to a distant village.

The great god Vishnu was watching over King Kans with disapproval. 'It is time to deal with Kans,' he decided. 'I will be reborn as his eighth child.'

Devaki soon gave birth to an eighth son, named Krishna. She and Vasudev gazed at their new-born baby, terrified that he too would soon be taken from them. But instead, Vishnu appeared before them, large and glowing.

'Take baby Krishna to the village of Gokul,' Vishnu ordered Vasudev. 'Exchange him for the new-born daughter of Yashodha and Nand Lal, the cowherd. King Kans has no reason to kill Devaki's daughter.'

Vasudev looked grimly at the chains on the door, but they fell away before his eyes and he walked through. Soon he arrived at the river Jamuna, which raged wildly, making it impossible to cross. Suddenly, a path appeared among the stormy waters before him. Clutching Krishna to him, Vasudev made his way to the cowherd's house.

Here, Vishnu helped out again. 'Vasudev will leave Krishna the child god for you to look after,' he told Yashodha and Nand. 'In return, your daughter will live with Vasudev and his wife Devaki like a princess.'

When Vishnu had gone, Yashodha and Nand forgot everything and believed Krishna to be their own son.

Krishna grew up in the countryside and the people from all around loved him dearly. He encouraged them to worship the god Vishnu instead of Indra, the protector of harvests. This infuriated Indra, who brought a rainstorm to punish the people. But Krishna lifted the huge mountain Govardhan and held it over the fields to shield their crops from the rain.

Kali, the Demon-slayer

Kali was a form of the
mother goddess, Parvati,
who was married to
Shiva. The two gods
often had contests with
each other. This story of
Kali in her most ferocious
form is one of the best-
known Indian myths.
It tells us how Kali
came to be created.

THE GIANTS SUMBHA AND NISUMBHA HAD
WORSHIPPED SHIVA FOR MANY CENTURIES AND, IN
RETURN FOR THEIR PRAYERS, HAD GAINED GREAT POWER.

'They boast they'll take over the world,' the gods
grumbled to Shiva. 'You must reduce their force.'

'I will do no such thing,' said Shiva. 'They have
earned their reward. But you could ask Parvati for help.
She is, after all, the Cosmic Mother.'

Parvati agreed to help. She protected the world and
would not let any giants take it over, even if they were
Shiva's devotees.

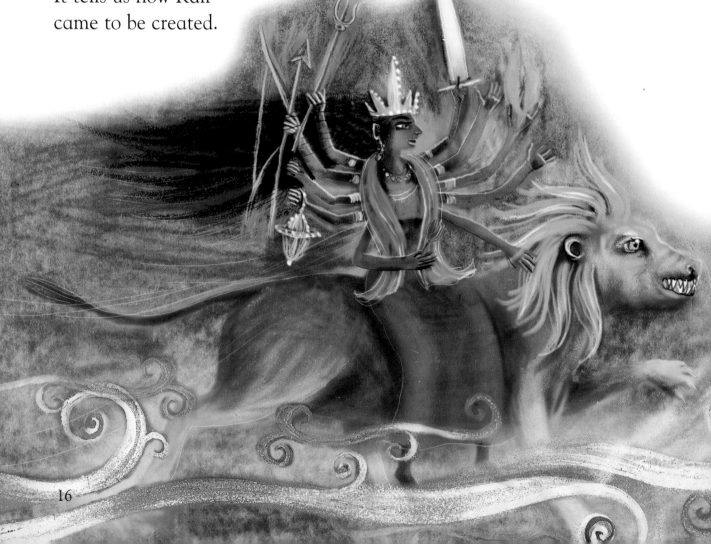

Parvati climbed to the highest peak of the Himalayan mountains and took the form of Durga, a beautiful woman riding a lion. The armies of Sumbha and Nisumbha saw Durga and attacked. But Durga was too powerful and cut them down almost instantly. The giants realised they were up against a huge force. They sent out their best general, Raktavij, against Durga, accompanied by his army of giants. Durga grew enormous and swirled her ten arms, holding many magical weapons. Soon Raktavij's warriors lay strewn on the ground and he was fighting Durga alone. But every time she attacked Raktavij, a thousand warriors sprang from each drop of his blood that touched the ground.

'Kali!' Durga called. Instantly, a massive black goddess emerged from her body and stood beside her. As Durga fought Raktavij, Kali caught the drops of his blood in her mouth, stopping them from turning into warriors. Soon, Raktavij was dead. Sumbha and Nisumbha were dead too. Kali stood amid the slain demons, wild with triumph. She stamped her feet and started turning. The world became a drum beneath her feet, beating out a victory tattoo. The gods and goddesses clapped. Urged on by the praise, Kali danced more wildly. Her energy made the world shake. The cries of praise turned to shouts of warning, but Kali danced on.

Shiva knew he had to intervene. He lay down among the dead demons. When Kali brought her foot down beside him, she felt Shiva's energy. With a shock, Kali stopped her wild dance. She realised she had saved the world from the giants, but had nearly destroyed it herself through pride.

The name Parvati means 'daughter of the mountain'. This goddess is worshipped as Durga by warriors, and as Kali and in her other fierce forms by those wishing to drive away fear and evil. She was first born as Sati, or Truth, to teach the world, but when her father insulted Shiva, she vanished into a fire and returned many centuries later as the goddess Parvati. She is much loved throughout India.

Ganesh

Ganesh is widely worshipped in India and by Hindus all over the world. He is the god of wisdom, and sacrifices are offered to him at the beginning of new projects because he is the remover of obstacles. He is plump and yellow-skinned and his carriage is drawn by a rat. There are many stories explaining why Ganesh has the head of an elephant.

THE GOD SHIVA AND HIS BEAUTIFUL WIFE PARVATI LIVED HIGH UP IN THE HIMALAYAN MOUNTAINS.

The two gods loved each other deeply, but Shiva spent much of his time praying and meditating far away from home, and Parvati was often lonely.

One hot day Parvati decided to bathe in a nearby lake. She swam vigorously, stretching out her arms and legs. As she swam, the dust from her body mixed with the water and formed a baby. Parvati scooped the infant into her arms. She was delighted! Now she had a companion, and when Shiva eventually returned from his meditations, they would be a family.

Parvati took the baby home, lay down with him in her arms and fell asleep gazing at him in wonder. But the baby, Ganesh, was no ordinary infant. As soon as he saw his mother asleep, he crept out of bed and over to the door to guard her bed chamber.

Soon, Shiva completed his meditations and strode back over the mountains to see his wife.

The little boy god barred his way. 'Who are you?' he asked.

Shiva was furious. Who was this small stranger to question him?

'Get out of my way,' he commanded.

But Ganesh raised his arm and held Shiva back. Shiva could not stand to be insulted, even by a little boy. With a mighty blow, he struck off Ganesh's head and marched in to his wife's bedroom.

'What have you done?' Parvati screamed. 'That was your son!'

'Did he not know I am the great Lord of Creation and Destruction?' Shiva bellowed furiously.

'How could he know?' wept Parvati. 'He was only just born.'

Instantly, Shiva was sorry for what he had done. He summoned his messengers, the demons, goblins, witches and sprites of Earth and air.

'Find a head for my son,' Shiva ordered.

Everywhere Shiva's creatures looked, they saw infants asleep, facing their mothers and they could not bear to behead them. At last, they found a baby elephant who had turned his back to his mother because his trunk was in the way. Immediately, they took his head and Shiva fixed it to Ganesh's body. The little god sat up, alive again. And that is how Ganesh came to have the head of an elephant.

The great sage Vyasa wanted to dictate a book to Ganesh, who agreed on the condition that Vyasa told his story without a single pause. The sage dictated 90,000 verses of 30 lines each. This book became the great epic known as the Mahabharata – the longest poem in the world. Because of this, many Indian writers pray to Ganesh at the start of each new book.

The Great War

This story comes from the beginning of the epic poem the Mahabharata, (The Great War). It tells the story of the war between the one hundred Kauravas and their cousins, the five Pandavas, over who would rule the kingdom of Kurujangal. Bhishma is the most important character of the epic, because he is present from start to finish as the protector of the hundred Kauravas.

King Shantanu pulled up his weary horse by the River Ganges. The river's pure waters would soothe his tiredness. As he splashed his face, he heard a tinkling noise and saw a beautiful woman bathing in the water. She wore a blue sari and glittering jewels and she was bathed in a strange glow.

'Who are you?' Shantanu asked.

'I am not of your world,' the woman replied.

But Shantanu was enchanted.

'Please marry me,' he begged.

'I will marry you,' the woman responded. 'But if you ever question my actions, I will leave you forever.'

Shantanu agreed to this condition and the entire kingdom celebrated the royal marriage. Soon, the queen gave birth to a son. Immediately, she walked to the window and hurled the baby into the rushing waters of the Ganges, saying, 'I do this for your own good.'

Shantanu was shattered, but he kept his promise. Six more times, the queen bore a boy and each time she fed it to the river with the same words. But when the eighth son came, Shantanu seized him from his mother's arms.

'Not this time,' he said. 'This son will live.'

'We could have been happy together with this son,' replied the queen sadly. 'But you have broken your promise and now I must go.'

Shantanu was heartbroken. 'Will you at least explain to me why you killed our sons?'

'I am Ganga, goddess of the river. The seven storm-gods were once cursed to be reborn as mortals. I could not prevent the curse, but I promised to release them from the cycle of rebirth. So I gave birth to each one and killed him before he sinned. Sinless and washed in my waters, they won't be reborn. This child is your heir. Call him Bhishma.'

Some say that the goddess Ganga sprang from the toe of Vishnu, while others claim that she was the daughter of Brahma. The story tells that she came down to Earth in the shape of the river Ganga (Ganges in English) because a king prayed for her to purify the wrong-doings of his ancestors. The Ganga is said to wash away the sins of her worshippers, even today.

Many years after Ganga had gone, Bhishma convinced his father to marry again. Shantanu's new queen was to be Satyavati, the daughter of a humble fisherman. But Satyavati's father was unhappy with the match.

Bhishma knew that the fisherman's real worry was that Satyavati's son could never be king, because Bhishma had first claim to the throne. But, knowing that his father had fallen in love with Satyavati, Bhishma decided to make a great sacrifice. That day when the court assembled, he summoned Satyavati and her father.

'I ask the sun, moon and stars to bear witness to my oath,' Bhishma declared. 'I will never be king of Kurujangal, nor will I father a child who can claim the throne.' He turned to Satyavati's father. 'Now do you agree to let your daughter marry my father?'

Shanatanu held up his hand. 'Take back your oath, my son, please,' he begged.

But Bhishma stood by his word.

'In that case,' said Shantanu sadly, 'may Yama let you live until you choose to die.'

And so it was that Bhishma lived to guide his nephews, the hundred Kauravas, until the Mahabharata finally reached its end.

The Rescue of Sita

This story about the kidnap and rescue of Sita is taken from the first epic, the Ramayana, which tells of the life of a great king, Rama of Ayodhya. Rama was cheated out of the throne by his evil stepmother, who insisted that Rama's father make her own son king and banish Rama and his wife Sita to the forest for fourteen years.

RAMA AND SITA LIVED HAPPILY IN A COTTAGE IN THE FOREST FOR MANY YEARS. One day when Rama was out hunting, Sita took pity on a poor old holy man and invited him into their home. Too late Sita realised her mistake, for the old man was the demon king Ravana in disguise. He bundled Sita into his chariot and flew her back to his kingdom on the island of Lanka.

Rama searched the forest for his wife for days, but with no success. At last, in desperation, he went to the monkey king for help. The monkey general, Hanuman, was entrusted with searching Lanka to find Sita. But he could not find her anywhere.

'Show me the way, Vishnu,' Hanuman prayed, closing his eyes. When he opened them, he saw a light glowing among some trees. Hanuman leapt towards it.

'Sita!' he exclaimed. 'Rama has sent me to find you.'

Sita's hair was tangled and her clothes hung about her in tatters. She was sick with grief and despair.

'Why has it taken Rama so long to find me?' asked Sita sadly. She handed Hanuman a jewel. 'This will prove you met me. Tell Rama if he does not come soon, I will be dead.'

Hanuman's fur glowed like a flame. He was furious with Sita's captor, Ravana. He said goodbye to Sita. And as a warning to Ravana, he destroyed as much of Lanka as he could.

'How dare this monkey attack us?' Ravana thundered, releasing 80,000 warrior demons against Hanuman. But the great monkey was the son of the wind-god Vayu and as powerful as a hurricane. He leapt nimbly out of the way of the demons and their weapons.

Furious, Ravana summoned his son Indrajit. 'Kill the monkey,' he commanded. 'Use the arrow Brahma gave you. It always hits its target.' Indrajit let loose his arrow and Hanuman fell to the ground, unconscious. Ravana's demons took him to their king. Ravana's ministers wrapped Hanuman's tail in cotton wool and oil and set it alight.

'That will show Rama what we think of him,' they sneered. As Hanuman's tail burst into flames, he leapt high into the air. But he had the protection of Agni, god of fire, and felt no pain. Hanuman flew on to Ravana's fort. Lashing wildly with his tail, he smashed its towers and set its walls on fire. Then he flew directly back to Rama and told him everything. Rama's army of monkeys and bears immediately made their way down to the sea.

'Build a bridge across to Lanka,' advised Sagar, the ocean-god. Very soon Rama's troops arrived in Ravana's city. But this time the demons were ready. They knew their city better than Rama and his army and they used magic to help them. Indrajit made himself invisible and shot Rama with his special arrow. Rama collapsed, unconscious. Jambavan, king of the bears, and Hanuman were skilled healers but they could not revive Rama. Still, they did not

give up hope. As evening fell, they heard the swish of wings and felt a strong gust of air. Out of the clouds came Garuda, the eagle who belonged to Vishnu.

'I come from my master,' Garuda said. 'Vishnu fights beside those who fight on the side of right.'

Garuda enclosed Rama in his mighty wings and when he released him, Rama stood up strong and healthy.

'Take my greetings to Sita,' Rama commanded Hanuman. 'Tell her she is safe.'

Rama's troops cheered. With Vishnu's help, they knew they would win the war.

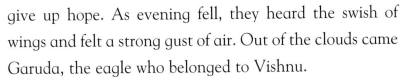

The first Indian epic, the Ramayana is read daily by many Hindus because it is said to wash away sin. According to legend, one of the Seven Sages, or Saptarishi, told a robber to repent by chanting the mantra 'ma-ra' until they returned. Seven years later, they returned to find him covered by an ant-hill, still chanting. They named him Valmiki, which means 'born from an ant-hill'. Later, Valmiki wrote down the story of the Ramayana as it unfolded before his eyes.

Death and the Healer

Yam-Raj, or Yama, is the god of death and lives with departed souls in Narg, the world of the dead. Some Hindus believe that he is the one who judges the sins of the dead and decides their punishment. When Yama goes to collect the soul from a dying body, he takes his mace and noose with him.

People are afraid of Yama because he is linked to death, but he is actually fair and kind. In one tale, he rewards a young woman who follows him past the stars and the sun to the gates of his kingdom, Narg, by returning her young husband to life. Yama is the son of Surya, the Sun.

ONCE, YAMA MARRIED A BEAUTIFUL MORTAL. Very soon, he found out that his wife had a terrible temper. When they had a son, Yama-Kumar, they battled constantly about how to bring him up.

'It's bad for the boy to see us arguing all the time,' Yama warned his wife. 'If it doesn't stop, I'll leave.' But that only started another fight, so Yama left.

Yama kept a fatherly eye on the boy as he grew. Things did not go well. Yama-Kumar grew into a lazy man with no idea of duty or prayer.

So Yama visited his son. 'If you promise to work hard, I will give you the sacred gift of healing,' he told him.

Yama-Kumar changed his ways. He worked hard, learning everything about herbs and other cures, and soon he mastered the skills of an excellent physician.

Yama was proud of the young healer and finally told him that he was his father. 'You have done well, my son,' he said. 'Here is my reward. I am always present at the sick bed. Look for me. If the patient can be healed, I will nod. But if I shake my head, the patient is incurable. You must explain that the patient is beyond help.'

'I will do as you say,' Yama-Kumar replied.

Yama-Kumar soon gained fame as an excellent physician, so when the king's daughter grew ill, he was naturally the one to be summoned to her bedside.

As usual, Yama-Kumar looked for his father. And there Yama stood, swinging his noose with one hand while he held his mace in the other. Grimly, he shook his head.

'Please let her live, Father,' Yama-Kumar begged.

'She is too young and well-loved to die.'

Yama did not like being challenged. But his son had never argued with him before, so he gave in. 'You have three days,' he hissed.

The healer thanked his father and began to tend the princess. He worked tirelessly and soon she was better. But Yama-Kumar knew this did not matter if Yama did not change his mind. As promised, Yama arrived on the third day. The healer looked up casually from his patient's bedside. 'Oh father,' he said, 'mother's been asking about you. Perhaps you'd be good enough to see her?'

Yama turned pale. 'Never!' he shuddered. 'Please, don't tell her where I am, or she'll follow me back to the land of the dead.'

Yama-Kumar laughed softly to himself. 'We can make a deal,' he offered. 'Leave the princess here and I promise to keep my mother away from you.'

When Yama had recovered from the shock, he chuckled. 'I like a man with wit. You can save your patient. She will live to be a very old lady.'

And so saying, he went about his business.

Trishankhu and the Sages

The Seven Sages (Saptarishi) were men of power and magic who often outdid the gods. But even they could not overturn the rules of heaven. The two sages in this story were deadly rivals. According to some Hindu writings, the Saptarishi still shine in the night sky in the constellation called the Ursa Major.

Surabhi emerged when the gods churned the Ocean of Milk. She had magical powers, and once helped the sage Vasishta by producing a troop of warriors to fight an evil king. Surabhi was also said to be able to grant all desires. It is probably because of her that cows are sacred to Hindus.

King Trishankhu wanted to go to Svarg, the heaven of the gods.

'If you atone for your sins, your soul will go there,' Vasishta, chief sage of the Saptarishi, told him.

Many years before, when Trishankhu was a young prince, he had abducted a woman from her home. His father had banished him from his kingdom for twelve years, saying, 'You can't simply take what you want.'

Trishankhu returned the woman to her home. While in exile in the forest, he tried hard to make amends. Every day he left food for the family of Vishvamitra, an old sage who was away on a mission. Then famine came. There were no animals to hunt and no berries or nuts to pick. The prince was so hungry that he killed Vasishta's cow, Surabhi, and ate her. Vasishta was grief-stricken.

'You will be known as Trishankhu from now on,' he cursed. 'He of the three sins. You abducted a woman, you killed a cow and you ate her flesh.'

When the twelve years of exile were over, Trishankhu returned to his kingdom. Soon, he inherited the throne.

'I will do my duty and advise the new king fairly,' the sage Vasishta decided. 'But I will never truly respect him.'

And now Trishankhu was once again showing the side of his character that Vasishta disliked.

'But I want to go to Svarg now,' Trishankhu sulked. 'Perform a ceremony. Make a sacrifice. Just get me to the heaven of the gods!'

Vasishta refused. This man could not simply demand

what he wanted. 'I will not insult the gods by breaking their laws.'

'Well then,' Trishankhu said, 'I'll ask Vishvamitra instead.'

Vishvamitra remembered Trishankhu's kindness to his family during his long years of exile. 'I'll do my best,' he promised. Vishvamitra lit a sacrificial fire and fed it many rich offerings. He chanted holy words, making the flames prance higher and higher. Suddenly, he pushed Trishankhu upwards. The king rose up on the flames, floating towards heaven.

But Indra, king of Svarg, held up a hand and Trishankhu hurtled back. Vishvamitra waved him up, and for a while Trishankhu tumbled back and forth between heaven and Earth.

'Stop!' bellowed Vishvamitra, suspending Trishankhu mid-heaven. 'Or I will create a new heaven for this man.'

Indra knew the old sage's power. He thought quickly. 'Can we leave Trishankhu where he is?'

Vishvamitra agreed and created a new constellation around the king. And to this day, Trishankhu shines brightly in the night sky.

Glossary

Agni – the god of fire.

Avatar – a god in human or animal form. Avatars would descend from heaven to Earth to help fight against evil.

Bhishma – the hero of the Mahabharata.

Brahma – the supreme god of creation. Along with Vishnu and Shiva, one of the famous triad of the gods of creation, survival and rebirth.

Chalice – a drinking cup or goblet.

Constellation – a group of stars that can be seen from the Earth.

Cosmos – the world or universe.

Dyaus-Pitar – the sky-god. Believed by the ancient Indians to be the father of creation.

Elixir (of Life) – a magical drink which was believed to prolong the life of those who drank it.

Epic – a long narrative poem, which traditionally describes the deeds of a legendary hero. Epics are often based on stories which have been passed down from one generation to another.

Ganesh – the god of wisdom and remover of obstacles. He is famous for having an elephant's head and was the son of Shiva and Parvati.

Ganga – the goddess of the sacred river Ganga (Ganges), which is believed to wash away the sins of those who bathe in its waters.

Hanuman – a brave general of the monkey army. He was the son of the wind-god, Vayu.

Indra – the supreme god of the ancient Indians. He was seen as the protector of harvests as he had the power to bring rain.

Krishna – the god of fields and hillsides. One of the avatars of the god Vishnu.

Lakshmi – the goddess of good fortune, created when the gods churned the Ocean of Milk. Wife of Vishnu.

Mahabharata – an epic poem which recounts the great war between two rival families over the throne of the kingdom of Kurujangal. It is over 100,000 verses long and was composed around 900 BCE.

Prithvi – the Earth goddess. Believed by ancient Indians to be the mother of creation.

Rama – a great king and hero of the first Indian epic, the Ramayana.

Ramayana – an epic poem which tells the story of the life of a great king, Rama of Ayodhya. The characters and events it describes are well-known in India to this day. It was written around 1000 BCE.

Rigveda – a collection of over a thousand hymns which tell of the early Vedic or nature gods, including Indra and Agni. They were written between 900 and 1500 BCE.

Sage – a wise man

Saptarishi – the seven powerful sages (wise men) of Indian mythology.

Sati-Parvati-Kali – the mother goddess. She appeared first as Sati and re-appeared hundreds of years later as Parvati. Kali is her most fierce form. She was married to Shiva and has many other forms such as Durga, the war-goddess.

Shiva – the god of destruction and rebirth.

Sita – the wife of Rama. The Ramayana describes her kidnap and rescue.

Surabhi – a magical cow, created when the gods and demons churned the Ocean of Milk. She had the ability to grant all wishes.

Surya – the sun-god.

Valmiki – the author of the Ramayana.

Vishnu – the preserver and protector of creation. It is believed that he will appear on Earth in ten different forms (called avatars) to help fight against evil; the seventh and eighth forms were Rama and Krishna, the tenth is yet to come.

Yama – the god of death.

Index